Contents

Answers

The 21st Century

1) Name the managers of Manchester City in the 21st Century from the dates given
   February 1998 – May 2001
   May 2001 – March 2005
   March 2005 – May 2007
   July 2007 – June 2008
   June 2008 – December 2009
   December 2009 – May 2013
   June 2013 – June 2016
   July 2016 – Present

2) Which player ended up in goal after Claudio Bravo was sent off against Atalanta in the Champions League in 2019?

3) Ben Thatcher was given an FA ban of eight games in 2006 after knocking out which opponent with an elbow?

4) Carlos Tevez caused a huge row after allegedly refusing to come on as a substitute against who in 2011?

5) Who scored after just 14 seconds in the 6-0 thrashing of Tottenham in 2013?

6) Mario Balotelli was substituted by manager Roberto Mancini after attempting to score with a backheel in a friendly against which side?

7) Manchester City conceded one of the quickest goals in Premier League history when which Newcastle player scored after just 10 seconds in their January 2003 encounter?

8) Who won the Premier League Golden Boot award for the 2014/15 season?

9) Which former Manchester City player was the first person to score 10 own goals in the Premier League?

10) Stuart Pearce infamously played David James up front the final part of a Premier League match against which team?

11) Who scored a hat trick in Manchester City's first home Premier League game of the 21st century in a 4-2 win over Sunderland?

Transfers

1) Which player joined from AC Milan in August 2000 before leaving to join Marseille just two months later?

2) Which centre back signed from Everton in 2000?

3) Which England international joined on a free from West Ham in 2001?

4) Which club did Paul Dickov leave to join in 2002?

5) Which former Manchester United player signed on a free in 2002?

6) Shaun Goater was sold to which team in 2003?

7) Which striker signed from Leeds in January 2003?

8) Manchester City bought midfielder Claudio Reyna from where in 2003?

9) Which goalkeeper signed from West Ham in 2004?

10) Which player did Manchester City sell to Fenerbahce in 2005?

11) Shaun Wright-Phillips moved to which English club in 2005?

12) Which goalkeeper was bought from Shrewsbury in 2006?

13) Nicky Weaver left Manchester City in 2007, moving to which club?

14) Vedran Corluka signed from which club in 2007?

15) Benjani was bought in January 2008 from where?

16) Paul Dickov left the club again in 2008 to join which club?

17) Future club captain Vincent Kompany signed in 2008 from which German team?

18) From which club did Pablo Zabaleta sign in 2008?

19) Sun Jihai left in 2008 to sign for which club?

20) For which club did Kasper Schmeichel sign after leaving Manchester City in 2009?

First Goals

1) Sergio Aguero

2) Robinho

3) Mario Balotelli

4) Micah Richards

5) Gabriel Jesus

6) Robbie Fowler

7) Shaun Wright-Phillips

8) Kevin De Bruyne

9) Yaya Toure

10) David Silva

11) Jon Macken

12) Bernardo Silva

Memorable Goals

1) Mario Balotelli scored an impudent goal with his shoulder against which team in December 2011?

2) Yaya Toure ran more than half the length of the field with the ball to cap off a 4-0 win over who in May 2014?

3) Which defender scored his only Man City goal as he blasted a strike in from 25 yards against Everton in October 2005?

4) Vincent Kompany scored with a vital long-range strike during the title run in against Leicester in 2019, which former Manchester City goalkeeper did he beat?

5) Who scored the second goal, smashing the ball into the roof of the net, in a 2-1 win over Aston Villa in May 2005?

6) Michael Johnson scored brilliantly with the outside of his foot in a 1-0 win over which team in August 2007?

7) Danilo scored with a thunderous right footed effort in February 2018 against which team?

8) Niclas Jensen hit an outrageous volley from the edge of the box against which side in 2003?

9) Sergio Aguero became Manchester City's all-time leading goal scorer when he netted his 178th goal against which side in 2017?

10) Which former Arsenal player ran the length of the pitch to mock their fans after he scored past them for Manchester City in 2009?

11) Who put City 1-0 ahead at Highbury in January 2005 with a sweetly struck long-range effort, before Arsenal came back to draw 1-1?

12) City won 2-1 in the Premier League in April 2013 after who came off the bench to score the winner, dancing past a number of defenders then firing the ball into the roof of the net?

Memorable Games

1) Manchester City clinched the Premier League title in the most dramatic of circumstances against Queens Park Rangers in 2012, but which former City player was sent off during the game?

2) Which three players scored for City against QPR on that dramatic day in 2012?

3) Manchester City won a crucial derby match against United in the closing weeks of the 2011/12 season, who scored the only goal of the game?

4) Who scored four goals as Man City beat Tottenham 5-1 away from home in August 2011?

5) Manchester City came from two goals down to win 3-2 at Norwich in 2005, who grabbed the last-minute winner?

6) City stunned Manchester United by winning 6-1 at Old Trafford in 2011, who was sent off for the hosts?

7) In that 6-1 victory who scored the 6th and final goal for City?

8) In the last ever Premier League Manchester derby at Maine Road, city won 3-1 and which player scored his 100th goal for the club?

9) City secured the 2013/14 Premier League title with a 2-0 win over which opponents on the last day of the season?

10) Sergio Aguero scored five times in a 6-1 win against which side in 2015?

11) City lost out to Tottenham in the race for fourth place in the 2009/10 season after who scored a winner for Spurs in the meeting between the sides in May?

12) City suffered their biggest ever Premier League loss when they were embarrassed by an 8-1 defeat to who in 2008?

13) Who scored the winner as Liverpool were crucially beaten 2-1 in January 2019?

14) Who did City beat on the last day of the 2018/19 season to secure the Premier League title?

15) City produced their biggest ever Premier League victory by beating which team 8-0 in September 2019?

The 21st Century II

1) In which season did Manchester City win 100 points in the Premier League?

2) City secured automatic promotion into the Premier League in 2000, finishing second in the table behind which club?

3) Who became City's oldest ever goal-scorer when he netted against Barnsley in October 2001?

4) What shirt number did Yaya Toure wear throughout his time at Manchester City?

5) City were relegated from the Premier League in 2001, which club sealed their fate by beating them 2-1 on May the 7th?

6) How many points did City pick up in the process of winning promotion back to the Premier League in the 2001/02 season?

7) In what year did Sheikh Mansour Bin Zayed Al Nahyan complete his takeover of Manchester City?

8) In what year did Manchester City player their final match at Maine Road?

9) City lost their final ever game at Maine Road to which team?

10) Who was the first scorer of a competitive goal at the City of Manchester Stadium (now known as the Etihad)?

11) City broke the record for the most team goals in a Premier League season when they scored how many during the 2017/18 campaign?

Transfers II

1) Which two players signed from Arsenal in July 2009?

2) Which defender signed for free from Barcelona in August 2009?

3) Which striker joined from Inter Milan in 2010?

4) Craig Bellamy left in August 2011 to join who?

5) From which club did Sergio Aguero sign in 2011?

6) Who signed on a free after leaving Manchester United in 2011?

7) Which future England defender left the club in January 2012 to join Burnley?

8) Defender Ben Mee was sold to which team in August 2012?

9) Carlos Tevez was sold to which club in 2013?

10) Which striker was bought from Swansea in 2015?

11) Scott Sinclair was sold to which team in June 2015?

12) Dedryck Boyata was sold in 2015 to who?

13) Who was bought from Wolfsburg in August 2015?

14) Which goalkeeper signed from Barcelona in 2016?

15) Jadon Sancho was sold to which German team in 2017?

16) Which player was purchased from Tottenham in 2017?

17) Yaya Toure left the club in 2018, signing for which team?

18) Which Premier League winning player signed for Manchester City in July 2018?

19) Which club did Vincent Kompany move to in 2019?

20) Which defender moved to Valencia in August 2019?

Cup Games

1) City won a sensational FA Cup tie in 2004, coming back from 3-0 down with ten men to beat Tottenham 4-3 with a last-minute winner headed in by which player?

2) Who played in goal for City during that remarkable match?

3) Who scored the only goal in the FA Cup final victory over Stoke in 2011?

4) What was the final score in the 2019 FA Cup final against Watford?

5) Which team beat City 1-0 at the third round stage of the 2004/05 FA Cup?

6) Who became the club's youngest ever goal-scorer in the 3-0 victory over Watford in the 2013 FA Cup third round?

7) Manchester City were on the wrong end of a huge upset when they lost 1-0 in the 2013 FA Cup final to which team?

8) Who knocked City of the FA Cup in the fifth round in 2018?

9) City lifted the League Cup in 2014 after defeating which opponents in the final?

10) Which goalkeeper was the hero when City won the League Cup on penalties in 2016?

11) Who scored City's only goal as the capitulated to a 5-1 loss to Chelsea in the fifth round of the 2015/16 FA Cup?

12) Arsenal were comfortably beaten in the 2018 League Cup final, which three City players scored in the 3-0 win?

13) Who scored the final penalty of the 2019 League Cup final shootout to see off Chelsea?

14) Man City knocked which team of out the League Cup on penalties in both 2017 and 2018?

15) Man City hammered Burton in the first leg of their League Cup semi-final by what score-line in 2019?

First Goals II

1) Joey Barton

2) Georgios Samaras

3) Darius Vassell

4) Elano

5) Craig Bellamy

6) Leroy Sane

7) Nicolas Anelka

8) Daniel Sturridge

9) Edin Dzeko

10) Owen Hargreaves

11) Benjani

12) Vincent Kompany

Red Cards

1) Who received his first career red card when he was sent off in the home game against Atalanta in the Champions League in 2019?

2) Who was dismissed in the FA Cup 3rd round tie versus Manchester United in 2012?

3) Mario Balotelli was sent off against which European opposition as City were knocked out of the Europa League in 2011?

4) In the 2008 2-1 loss to Tottenham, which two Manchester City players were sent off?

5) Which player was sent off during the 1-0 win over Wigan in January 2009?

6) Vincent Kompany was sent off during a 2-0 win against which team in January 2013?

7) Who was sent off during the 1-0 defeat to Arsenal in April 2012?

8) Who was sent off as City were eliminated from the UEFA Cup in 2009 by Hamburg?

9) Who saw red in the 1-1 draw with Blackburn in November 2004?

10) Which player was sent off after coming on as a substitute in the 1-1 draw with Liverpool in November 2011?

11) Who was dismissed alongside Bacary Sagna after the pair clashed in the January 2011 match with Arsenal?

12) Which City player was sent off against his former club during a 2-1 loss to Arsenal in February 2004?

13) How many times was Richard Dunne sent off in his Manchester City career?

European Games

1) Manchester City lost 3-1 to which polish side in the Europa League group stage in 2010?

2) In what unusual way did City qualify to play in the 2003/04 UEFA Cup?

3) Which team did Man City beat 5-0 in the first competitive game at their new stadium, then known as the City of Manchester Stadium?

4) In 2008 City played a European home game at which ground while their own pitch was being re-laid?

5) Which club were Manchester City knocked out by in the Champions League knockout stages in both 2014 and 2015?

6) Who scored the equaliser as City drew 1-1 away with Juventus in the Europa League group stage in 2010?

7) Who were Manchester City's opponents in their first ever Champions League match in 2011?

8) Which club knocked City out of the Champions League at the semi-final stage in 2016?

9) Who controversially scored the final goal of the tie as Tottenham knocked City out of the Champions League on away goals in 2019?

10) What was the score of the second leg of Man City's knockout tie against Schalke in the Champions League in 2019?

The 21st Century Answers

1) Name the managers of Manchester City in the 21st Century from the dates given
   Joe Royle February 1998 – May 2001
   Kevin Keegan May 2001 – March 2005
   Stuart Pearce March 2005 – May 2007
   Sven-Goran Eriksson July 2007 – June 2008
   Mark Hughes June 2008 – December 2009
   Roberto Mancini December 2009 – May 2013
   Manuel Pellegrini June 2013 – June 2016
   Pep Guardiola July 2016 – Present

2) Which player ended up in goal after Claudio Bravo was sent off against Atalanta in the Champions League in 2019?
   Kyle Walker

3) Ben Thatcher was given an FA ban of eight games in 2006 after knocking out which opponent with an elbow?
Pedro Mendes

4) Carlos Tevez caused a huge row after allegedly refusing to come on as a substitute against who in 2011?
Bayern Munich

5) Who scored after just 14 seconds in the 6-0 thrashing of Tottenham in 2013?
Jesus Navas

6) Mario Balotelli was substituted by manager Roberto Mancini after attempting to score with a backheel in a friendly against which side?
LA Galaxy

7) Manchester City conceded one of the quickest goals in Premier League history when which Newcastle player scored after just 10 seconds in their January 2003 encounter?
Alan Shearer

8) Who won the Premier League Golden Boot award for the 2014/15 season?
Sergio Aguero

9) Which former Manchester City player was the first person to score 10 own goals in the Premier League?
Richard Dunne

10) Stuart Pearce infamously played David James up front the final part of a Premier League match against which team?
Middlesbrough

11) Who scored a hat trick in Manchester City's first home Premier League game of the 21st century in a 4-2 win over Sunderland?
Paulo Wanchope

Transfers Answers

1) Which player joined from AC Milan in August 2000 before leaving to join Marseille just two months later?
George Weah

2) Which centre back signed from Everton in 2000?
Richard Dunne

3) Which England international joined on a free from West Ham in 2001?
Stuart Pearce

4) Which club did Paul Dickov leave to join in 2002?
Leicester City

5) Which former Manchester United player signed on a free in 2002?
Peter Schmeichel

6) Shaun Goater was sold to which team in 2003?
Reading

7) Which striker signed from Leeds in January 2003?
Robbie Fowler

8) Manchester City bought midfielder Claudio Reyna from where in 2003?
Sunderland

9) Which goalkeeper signed from West Ham in 2004?
David James

10) Which player did Manchester City sell to Fenerbahce in 2005?
Nicolas Anelka

11) Shaun Wright-Phillips moved to which English club in 2005?
Chelsea

12) Which goalkeeper was bought from Shrewsbury in 2006?
Joe Hart

13) Nicky Weaver left Manchester City in 2007, moving to which club?
Charlton Athletic

14) Vedran Corluka signed from which club in 2007?
Dinamo Zagreb

15) Benjani was bought in January 2008 from where?
Portsmouth

16) Paul Dickov left the club again in 2008 to join which club?
Leicester City

17) Future club captain Vincent Kompany signed in 2008 from which German team?
Hamburg

18) From which club did Pablo Zabaleta sign in 2008?
Espanyol

19) Sun Jihai left in 2008 to sign for which club?
Sheffield United

20) For which club did Kasper Schmeichel sign after leaving Manchester City in 2009?
Notts County

First Goals – Name the clubs these players scored their first Manchester City goals against

1) Sergio Aguero
   Swansea City

2) Robinho
   Chelsea

3) Mario Balotelli
   Politehnica Timisoara

4) Micah Richards
   Aston Villa

5) Gabriel Jesus
   West Ham

6) Robbie Fowler
   Birmingham City

7) Shaun Wright-Phillips
   Millwall

8) Kevin De Bruyne
   West Ham

9) Yaya Toure
   Wigan Athletic

10) David Silva
    RB Salzburg

11) Jon Macken
    Bradford City

12) Bernardo Silva
    Stoke City

Memorable Goals Answers

1) Mario Balotelli scored an impudent goal with his shoulder against which team in December 2011?
Norwich City

2) Yaya Toure ran more than half the length of the field with the ball to cap off a 4-0 win over who in May 2014?
Aston Villa

3) Which defender scored his only Man City goal as he blasted a strike in from 25 yards against Everton in October 2005?
Danny Mills

4) Vincent Kompany scored with a vital long-range strike during the title run in against Leicester in 2019, which former Manchester City goalkeeper did he beat?
Kasper Schmeichel

5) Who scored the second goal, smashing the ball into the roof of the net, in a 2-1 win over Aston Villa in May 2005?
Kiki Musampa

6) Michael Johnson scored brilliantly with the outside of his foot in a 1-0 win over which team in August 2007?
Derby County

7) Danilo scored with a thunderous right footed effort in February 2018 against which team?
Burnley

8) Niclas Jensen hit an outrageous volley from the edge of the box against which side in 2003?
Leeds United

9) Sergio Aguero became Manchester City's all-time leading goal scorer when he netted his 178th goal against which side in 2017?
Napoli

10) Which former Arsenal player ran the length of the pitch to mock their fans after he scored past them for Manchester City in 2009?
Emmanuel Adebayor

11) Who put City 1-0 ahead at Highbury in January 2005 with a sweetly struck long-range effort, before Arsenal came back to draw 1-1?
Shaun Wright-Phillips

12) City won 2-1 in the Premier League in April 2013 after who came off the bench to score the winner, dancing past a number of defenders then firing the ball into the roof of the net?
Sergio Aguero

Memorable Games Answers

1) Manchester City clinched the Premier League title in the most dramatic of circumstances against Queens Park Rangers in 2012, but which former City player was sent off during the game?
Joey Barton

2) Which three players scored for City against QPR on that dramatic day in 2012?
Pablo Zabaleta, Edin Dzeko and Sergio Aguero

3) Manchester City won a crucial derby match against United in the closing weeks of the 2011/12 season, who scored the only goal of the game?
Vincent Kompany

4) Who scored four goals as Man City beat Tottenham 5-1 away from home in August 2011?
Edin Dzeko

5) Manchester City came from two goals down to win 3-2 at Norwich in 2005, who grabbed the last-minute winner?
Robbie Fowler

6) City stunned Manchester United by winning 6-1 at Old Trafford in 2011, who was sent off for the hosts?
Jonny Evans

7) In that 6-1 victory who scored the 6th and final goal for City?
Edin Dzeko

8) In the last ever Premier League Manchester derby at Maine Road, city won 3-1 and which player scored his 100th goal for the club?
Shaun Goater

9) City secured the 2013/14 Premier League title with a 2-0 win over which opponents on the last day of the season?
West Ham

10) Sergio Aguero scored five times in a 6-1 win against which side in 2015?
Newcastle United

11) City lost out to Tottenham in the race for fourth place in the 2009/10 season after who scored a winner for Spurs in the meeting between the sides in May?
Peter Crouch

12) City suffered their biggest ever Premier League loss when they were embarrassed by an 8-1 defeat to who in 2008?
Middlesbrough

13) Who scored the winner as Liverpool were crucially beaten 2-1 in January 2019?
Leroy Sane

14) Who did City beat on the last day of the 2018/19 season to secure the Premier League title?
Brighton

15) City produced their biggest ever Premier League victory by beating which team 8-0 in September 2019?

Watford

The 21st Century II Answers

1) In which season did Manchester City win 100 points in the Premier League?
2017/18

2) City secured automatic promotion into the Premier League in 2000, finishing second in the table behind which club?
Charlton Athletic

3) Who became City's oldest ever goal-scorer when he netted against Barnsley in October 2001?
Stuart Pearce

4) What shirt number did Yaya Toure wear throughout his time at Manchester City?
42

5) City were relegated from the Premier League in 2001, which club sealed their fate by beating them 2-1 on May the 7th?
Ipswich Town

6) How many points did City pick up in the process of winning promotion back to the Premier League in the 2001/02 season?

99

7) In what year did Sheikh Mansour Bin Zayed Al Nahyan complete his takeover of Manchester City?

2008

8) In what year did Manchester City player their final match at Maine Road?

2003

9) City lost their final ever game at Maine Road to which team?

Southampton

10) Who was the first scorer of a competitive goal at the City of Manchester Stadium (now known as the Etihad)?

Trevor Sinclair

11) City broke the record for the most team goals in a Premier League season when they scored how many during the 2017/18 campaign?

106

Transfers II Answers

1) Which two players signed from Arsenal in July 2009?
Emmanuel Adebayor and Kolo Toure

2) Which defender signed for free from Barcelona in August 2009?
Slyvinho

3) Which striker joined from Inter Milan in 2010?
Mario Balotelli

4) Craig Bellamy left in August 2011 to join who?
Liverpool

5) From which club did Sergio Aguero sign in 2011?
Athletico Madrid

6) Who signed on a free after leaving Manchester United in 2011?
Owen Hargreaves

7) Which future England defender left the club in January 2012 to join Burnley?
Kieran Trippier

8) Defender Ben Mee was sold to which team in August 2012?
Burnley

9) Carlos Tevez was sold to which club in 2013?
Juventus

10) Which striker was bought from Swansea in 2015?
Wilfried Bony

11) Scott Sinclair was sold to which team in June 2015?
Aston Villa

12) Dedryck Boyata was sold in 2015 to who?
Celtic

13) Who was bought from Wolfsburg in August 2015?
Kevin De Bruyne

14) Which goalkeeper signed from Barcelona in 2016?
Claudio Bravo

15) Jadon Sancho was sold to which German team in 2017?
Borussia Dortmund

16) Which player was purchased from Tottenham in 2017?
Kyle Walker

17) Yaya Toure left the club in 2018, signing for which team?
Olympiakos

18) Which Premier League winning player signed for Manchester City in July 2018?
Riyad Mahrez

19) Which club did Vincent Kompany move to in 2019?

Anderlecht

20) Which defender moved to Valencia in August 2019?

Eliaquim Mangala

Cup Games Answers

1) City won a sensational FA Cup tie in 2004, coming back from 3-0 down with ten men to beat Tottenham 4-3 with a last-minute winner headed in by which player?
Jon Macken

2) Who played in goal for City during that remarkable match?
Arni Arason

3) Who scored the only goal in the FA Cup final victory over Stoke in 2011?
Yaya Toure

4) What was the final score in the 2019 FA Cup final against Watford?
6-0

5) Which team beat City 1-0 at the third round stage of the 2004/05 FA Cup?
Oldham Athletic

6) Who became the club's youngest ever goal-scorer in the 3-0 victory over Watford in the 2013 FA Cup third round?
Rony Lopes

7) Manchester City were on the wrong end of a huge upset when they lost 1-0 in the 2013 FA Cup final to which team?
Wigan Athletic

8) Who knocked City of the FA Cup in the fifth round in 2018?
Wigan Athletic

9) City lifted the League Cup in 2014 after defeating which opponents in the final?
Sunderland

10) Which goalkeeper was the hero when City won the League Cup on penalties in 2016?
Willy Caballero

11) Who scored City's only goal as the capitulated to a 5-1 loss to Chelsea in the fifth round of the 2015/16 FA Cup?
David Faupala

12) Arsenal were comfortably beaten in the 2018 League Cup final, which three City players scored in the 3-0 win?
Sergio Aguero, Vincent Kompany and David Silva

13) Who scored the final penalty of the 2019 League Cup final shootout to see off Chelsea?
Raheem Sterling

14) Man City knocked which team of out the League Cup on penalties in both 2017 and 2018?
Leicester City

15) Man City hammered Burton in the first leg of their League Cup semi-final by what score-line in 2019?
9-0

First Goals II Answers

1) Joey Barton
   Tottenham Hotspur

2) Georgios Samaras
   Charlton Athletic

3) Darius Vassell
   Sunderland

4) Elano
   Newcastle United

5) Craig Bellamy
   Newcastle United

6) Leroy Sane
   Arsenal

7) Nicolas Anelka
   Everton

8) Daniel Sturridge
   Sheffield United

9) Edin Dzeko
   Notts County

10) Owen Hargreaves
    Birmingham City

11) Benjani
    Manchester United

12) Vincent Kompany
    Wigan Athletic

Red Cards Answers

1) Who received his first career red card when he was sent off in the home game against Atalanta in the Champions League in 2019?
Phil Foden

2) Who was dismissed in the FA Cup 3rd round tie versus Manchester United in 2012?
Vincent Kompany

3) Mario Balotelli was sent off against which European opposition as City were knocked out of the Europa League in 2011?
Dynamo Kiev

4) In the 2008 2-1 loss to Tottenham, which two Manchester City players were sent off?
Gelson Fernandes and Richard Dunne

5) Which player was sent off during the 1-0 win over Wigan in January 2009?
Richard Dunne

6) Vincent Kompany was sent off during a 2-0 win against which team in January 2013?
Arsenal

7) Who was sent off during the 1-0 defeat to Arsenal in April 2012?
Mario Balotelli

8) Who was sent off as City were eliminated from the UEFA Cup in 2009 by Hamburg?
Richard Dunne

9) Who saw red in the 1-1 draw with Blackburn in November 2004?
Danny Mills

10) Which player was sent off after coming on as a substitute in the 1-1 draw with Liverpool in November 2011?
Mario Balotelli

11) Who was dismissed alongside Bacary Sagna after the pair clashed in the January 2011 match with Arsenal?
Pablo Zabaleta

12) Which City player was sent off against his former club during a 2-1 loss to Arsenal in February 2004?
Nicolas Anelka

13) How many times was Richard Dunne sent off in his Manchester City career?
7

European Games Answers

1) Manchester City lost 3-1 to which polish side in the Europa League group stage in 2010?
Lech Poznan

2) In what unusual way did City qualify to play in the 2003/04 UEFA Cup?
The Fair Play Award

3) Which team did Man City beat 5-0 in the first competitive game at their new stadium, then known as the City of Manchester Stadium?
Welsh side TNS

4) In 2008 City played a European home game at which ground while their own pitch was being re-laid?
Oakwell – Home of Barnsley

5) Which club were Manchester City knocked out by in the Champions League knockout stages in both 2014 and 2015?
Barcelona

6) Who scored the equaliser as City drew 1-1 away with Juventus in the Europa League group stage in 2010?
Jo

7) Who were Manchester City's opponents in their first ever Champions League match in 2011?
Napoli

8) Which club knocked City out of the Champions League at the semi-final stage in 2016?
Real Madrid

9) Who controversially scored the final goal of the tie as Tottenham knocked City out of the Champions League on away goals in 2019?
Fernando Llorente

10) What was the score of the second leg of Man City's knockout tie against Schalke in the Champions League in 2019?
7-0

Printed in Great Britain
by Amazon